Attributing Biological Weapons Use

Strengthening Department of Defense
Capabilities to Investigate Deliberate
Biological Incidents

TRACEY RISSMAN, ANNETTE PRIETO

NATIONAL DEFENSE RESEARCH INSTITUTE

For more information on this publication, visit **www.rand.org/t/RRA2360-1**.

About RAND

The RAND Corporation is a research organization that develops solutions to public policy challenges to help make communities throughout the world safer and more secure, healthier and more prosperous. RAND is nonprofit, nonpartisan, and committed to the public interest. To learn more about RAND, visit www.rand.org.

Research Integrity

Our mission to help improve policy and decisionmaking through research and analysis is enabled through our core values of quality and objectivity and our unwavering commitment to the highest level of integrity and ethical behavior. To help ensure our research and analysis are rigorous, objective, and nonpartisan, we subject our research publications to a robust and exacting quality-assurance process; avoid both the appearance and reality of financial and other conflicts of interest through staff training, project screening, and a policy of mandatory disclosure; and pursue transparency in our research engagements through our commitment to the open publication of our research findings and recommendations, disclosure of the source of funding of published research, and policies to ensure intellectual independence. For more information, visit www.rand.org/about/principles.

RAND's publications do not necessarily reflect the opinions of its research clients and sponsors.

Published by the RAND Corporation, Santa Monica, Calif.
© 2024 RAND Corporation
RAND® is a registered trademark.

Library of Congress Cataloging-in-Publication Data is available for this publication.

ISBN: 978-1-9774-1288-1

Cover: SrdjanPav/Getty Images.

Limited Print and Electronic Distribution Rights

About This Report

In this foundational report, we analyze issues related to attributing biological weapons (BW) use and identify areas in which the U.S. Department of Defense (DoD) could enhance its capabilities to support U.S. efforts in investigating alleged BW uses and, thus, strengthening the United Nations (UN) Secretary-General's Mechanism for Investigation of Alleged Use of Chemical and Biological Weapons (UNSGM). We reviewed U.S. government and international policy documents and scientific and other open-source literature to answer the following research questions:

- Why is attribution of BW use important?
- During a biological incident, including BW use, what evidence might provide valuable information to facilitate attribution?
- What is the state of the science for determining the origin of a biological incident, including BW use?
- What capabilities does DoD possess or could it develop to facilitate attribution of BW use?

Determining the cause and source of biological incidents is difficult, particularly in identifying actors that could have deliberately caused such events through BW use. The *National Biodefense Strategy and Implementation Plan for Countering Biological Threats, Enhancing Pandemic Preparedness, and Achieving Global Health Security* has designated DoD with a lead role in strengthening the capabilities of the UNSGM. The National Biodefense Strategy and Implementation Plan (NBS) includes strengthening the UNSGM as an action that can contribute to BW deterrence by supporting international efforts to hold actors accountable for BW development, proliferation, and use. Further research and analysis could help prioritize in which areas it would be most beneficial for DoD to concentrate its efforts and help identify specific actions DoD could take to make progress in these areas.

The research reported here was completed in July 2023 and underwent security review with the sponsor and the Defense Office of Prepublication and Security Review before public release.

RAND National Security Research Division

This research was conducted within the International Security and Defense Policy Program of the RAND National Security Research Division (NSRD), which operates the National Defense Research Institute (NDRI), a federally funded research and development center sponsored by the Office of the Secretary of Defense, the Joint Staff, the Unified Combatant Commands, the Navy, the Marine Corps, the defense agencies, and the defense intelligence enterprise.

For more information on the RAND International Security and Defense Policy Program, see www.rand.org/nsrd/isdp or contact the director (contact information is provided on the webpage).

Acknowledgments

We are grateful to Michael Spirtas and John Parachini for proposing this project and for their support and guidance throughout. We also would like to thank Hayley Severance, Sara Duhachek Muggy, Jim Powers, and Heather Williams for taking time to review this report and provide invaluable feedback. Their thoughtful and thorough comments greatly enhanced the final product.

Summary

The White House has given the U.S. Department of Defense (DoD) a lead role in U.S. efforts to strengthen the United Nations (UN) Secretary-General's Mechanism for Investigation of Alleged Use of Chemical and Biological Weapons (UNSGM). One way for DoD to help enhance the UNSGM's capability to investigate alleged biological weapons (BW) uses is to strengthen the United States' capabilities in this area, particularly the ability to attribute BW use to the actor (or actors) responsible. Stronger U.S. capabilities can better enable the UNSGM (the only international body in this role) to investigate and attribute alleged BW use, even in instances in which the United States was not the target. The People's Republic of China (PRC), Iran, the Democratic Republic of Korea (DPRK), and Russia already present potential BW threats, and nonstate actors present an added threat. Advances in dual-use biological technology over the next several years could enable development of novel BW agents or delivery methods that could complicate detection of BW agents, attribution of BW attacks, and medical treatment of injuries or diseases caused by exposure to BW agents. Such advances provide imperatives for the United States and its allies to enhance capabilities to investigate alleged BW uses. However, these advances also provide opportunities in the form of tools that facilitate investigations.

International mechanisms to prevent and respond to BW are less robust than those for chemical weapons (CW). There is no BW counterpart to the Organization for the Prohibition of Chemical Weapons (OPCW), which provides an implementing body for the Chemical Weapons Convention, a central repository of CW experts, and analytical laboratories to provide technical support. Although the UN's Office for Disarmament Affairs has been working to identify BW laboratory capabilities and experts it can draw on from member states, it does not have parallel in-house capabilities nor does it enjoy the international credibility that the OPCW has garnered from successful past investigations. Investigating and attributing biological incidents can present additional complexities in detection and confirming a deliberative versus natural event. Even four years after the coronavirus disease 2019 pandemic, the U.S. Intelligence Community has differing assessments on its origins.

Attribution of BW use is important for reasons beyond holding actors responsible. Developing and maintaining robust capabilities and processes to conduct investigations of BW use can provide a deterrent against their use, improve understanding of adversaries' BW-related capabilities and doctrines, and inform improvements to biodefense capabilities. In this report, we delineate the stages at which evidence could be collected prior to, during, and after a biological incident to inform investigations and the collection and handling mechanisms for that evidence to facilitate attribution. The United States should also be attuned to key indicators we identify that could suggest a biological incident is deliberate. We find that there are opportunities for DoD specifically to enhances its capabilities in this area, such as the following:

- **Enhance and build flexibility and redundancy, as appropriate, into DoD's processes and capabilities to investigate and attribute biological incidents.** Determining attribution can be difficult, but developing and maintaining robust capabilities and processes to conduct investigations of BW use and determine the actor(s) responsible are an important part of reinforcing international norms against BW use. Investigators can draw more-confident attribution conclusions when they have more high-quality information from a variety of sources that provides insights into different aspects of the biological incident.
- **Continue to invest in biotechnology, including microbial forensic technology.** Identifying that a biological incident occurred and determining the origin or establishing attribution require a range of technical capabilities.
- **Maintain transparency about DoD efforts to work with international partners on biosecurity and biodefense efforts.** U.S. adversaries could wage disinformation campaigns about U.S. biosecurity and biodefense efforts worldwide to discredit UNSGM investigations of BW use and their conclusions, especially if UNSGM reports include attribution assessments.

Contents

Figure and Tables

Figure

Tables

Introduction

In this report, we address how the U.S. Department of Defense (DoD) could lead and contribute to the U.S. government's efforts to strengthen the United Nations (UN) Secretary-General's Mechanism for Investigation of Alleged Use of Chemical and Biological Weapons (UNSGM) to determine the facts, including those related to attribution, regarding the alleged use of BW, including toxin weapons. We do so by addressing the following research questions:

- Why is attribution of BW, including toxin weapons, use important?
- During a biological incident, including BW use, what evidence might provide valuable information to facilitate attribution?
- What is the state of the science for determining the origin of a biological incident, including BW use?
- What capabilities does DoD possess or could it develop to facilitate attribution of BW use?

The importance of this issue is highlighted in the *National Biodefense Strategy and Implementation Plan for Countering Biological Threats, Enhancing Pandemic Preparedness, and Achieving Global Health Security*, which the White House published in October 2022 to outline the U.S. government's approach to counter the full range of possibly catastrophic biological incidents,[1] whether natural, accidental, or deliberate. The National Biodefense Strategy and Implementation Plan (NBS) outlines goals and objectives for strengthening the biodefense enterprise,[2] which comprises all

---

[1] The NBS defines *biological incidents*, or *bioincidents*, as "any natural or accidental occurrence in which a biothreat harms humans, animals, plants, or the environment," "any crime involving a biothreat," or "any act of biological warfare or terrorism" (White House, *National Biodefense Strategy and Implementation Plan for Countering Biological Threats, Enhancing Pandemic Preparedness, and Achieving Global Health Security*, p. 14).

[2] The NBS defines *biodefense* as "actions to counter biological threats, reduce biological risks, and prepare for, respond to, and recover from bioincidents, whether naturally occurring, accidental, or deliberate in origin and whether impacting human, animal, plant, or environmental health" (White House, *National Biodefense Strategy and Imple-*

stakeholders—including federal and state, local, tribal, and territorial governments; nongovernmental and private sector entities; and international partners—that have roles in "assessing, preventing, preparing for, responding to, and recovering from" biological incidents.[3] The NBS states that the mission of the U.S. government during a biological incident is to "save lives; reduce human and animal suffering; protect property and the environment; control the spread of disease; support community efforts to overcome the physical, emotional, environmental, and economic impact of the incident; and determine the cause and source of the incident."[4] In its implementation plan, the NBS identifies priorities and target areas for each objective and assigns U.S. government departments and agencies, including DoD, to lead and support roles for actions related to each target area.[5]

In this report, we concentrate on deliberate biological incidents caused by the use of BW, including toxin weapons, and U.S. government and international efforts to attribute (or determine the actors responsible for) BW use. Specifically, we focus on DoD's roles and capabilities related to the NBS-specified action to "strengthen the capability of the UN Secretary-General's Mechanism for Investigation of Alleged Use of Chemical and Biological Weapons (UNSGM) to determine the facts, including attribution, regarding the alleged use of biological or toxin weapons" (NBS Goal 2, Priority 2.2, Target 2.2.4, Action III). The NBS designates DoD, the U.S. Department of State (DoS), and the Federal Bureau of Investigation (FBI) as co-leads for related U.S. government activities for this action. We reviewed U.S. government and international policy documents and scientific and other open-

---

mentation Plan for Countering Biological Threats, Enhancing Pandemic Preparedness, and Achieving Global Health Security, p. 14).

[3] White House, National Biodefense Strategy and Implementation Plan for Countering Biological Threats, Enhancing Pandemic Preparedness, and Achieving Global Health Security, p. 5.

[4] White House, National Biodefense Strategy and Implementation Plan for Countering Biological Threats, Enhancing Pandemic Preparedness, and Achieving Global Health Security, p. 5.

[5] White House, National Biodefense Strategy and Implementation Plan for Countering Biological Threats, Enhancing Pandemic Preparedness, and Achieving Global Health Security.

source literature to address how DoD can lead and contribute to this NBS action. See the appendix for other NBS actions for which DoD has lead roles.

BW threats remain a worldwide concern, and the UNSGM is the only international mechanism for investigating alleged BW use.[6] The international community would most likely face procedural, capability-related, and political challenges in launching the UNSGM to investigate and attribute allegations of BW use. The United States continues to address these challenges through political channels and multilateral fora, and it could also do so by strengthening its own capabilities in support of the overall mission of the UNSGM. The NBS includes an action to strengthen the capability of the UNSGM, which the NBS highlights could deter BW use by providing a robust, unbiased process to determine the facts, including those related to culpability, of alleged BW uses. Developing and strengthening U.S. government capabilities to collect and analyze evidence—including interviews and physiological and environmental samples—during and after alleged BW use would serve to support and strengthen the UNSGM. The UNSGM guidelines and procedures note that member states can "bring a report of alleged use to the Secretary-General's attention to enable him to carry out an investigation, as warranted," and they continue that "[s]uch a report should be accompanied by relevant information supporting its validity,"[7] which would be best demonstrated by providing the most robust and complete information available. The UNSGM states that "[t]he Secretary-General should not be precluded from using additional information that may be brought to his attention by any other Member State on any aspect of possible use that would facilitate the conduct of the investigation,"[8] indicating that the

---

[6] United Nations Office for Disarmament Affairs (UNODA), "Secretary-General's Mechanism for Investigation of Alleged Use of Chemical and Biological Weapons (UNSGM)"; UNODA, "Fact Sheet: The Secretary-General's Mechanism for Investigation of Alleged Use of Chemical and Biological Weapons"; Switzerland Federal Department of Defense Spiez Laboratory, *UNSGM Designated Laboratories Workshop Report.*

[7] United Nations General Assembly (UNGA) Document A/44/561, *Chemical and Bacteriological (Biological) Weapons Report of the Secretary-General*; Green, "The Mechanisms Behind the United Nations Secretary-General's Mechanism," p. 12.

[8] UNGA Document A/44/561, *Chemical and Bacteriological (Biological) Weapons Report of the Secretary-General*; Green, "The Mechanisms Behind the United Nations Secretary-General's Mechanism," p. 13.

United States could share information regarding an alleged BW use even if not involved directly with requesting the UNSGM investigation.

BW Threats Continue and Are Increasing

The deliberate use of biological agents or toxins as BW to harm humans, animals, plants, or the environment represents a persistent and possibly growing threat to U.S. interests at home and abroad from both state and nonstate actors. The UNSGM's purpose does not specifically cover use of chemical and biological weapons (CBW) by nonstate actors, but member states can request an investigation of any alleged CBW use.

The United States is concerned that the People's Republic of China (PRC), Iran, the Democratic Republic of Korea (DPRK), and Russia are conducting activities possibly related to offensive BW purposes (see Table 1).[9] The U.S. Intelligence Community (IC) has postulated that

> global shortcomings in preparedness for the [coronavirus disease 2019] COVID-19 pandemic and concerns with biosecurity, fabricated public claims about U.S. biological weapons development fueled by U.S. adversaries, as well as continued questions surrounding the origins of the COVID-19 virus, may inspire some adversaries to consider options related to the development of biological weapons.[10]

Advances in dual-use biological technology over the next several years could enable the development of novel BW agents or delivery methods that complicate detection of BW agents, attribution of BW attacks, and medical treatment of injuries or diseases caused by exposure to BW agents.[11]

In 2022, the IC assessed that some state and nonstate actors "remain interested in using chemical and biological agents in attacks against U.S. interests and possibly the U.S. homeland."[12] Nonstate actors—for example,

---

[9] DoS, *Adherence to and Compliance with Arms Control, Nonproliferation, and Disarmament Agreements and Commitments.*

[10] U.S. Office of the Director of National Intelligence (ODNI), *Annual Threat Assessment of the U.S. Intelligence Community,* 2023, p. 25.

[11] ODNI, *Annual Threat Assessment of the U.S. Intelligence Community,* 2023.

[12] ODNI, *Annual Threat Assessment of the U.S. Intelligence Community,* 2022, p. 26.

TABLE 1

U.S. BW-Related Assessments for State Actors

State Actor	U.S. BW-Related Assessments
PRC	The United States assesses that "the PRC possessed an offensive BW program from the early 1950s to at least the late 1980s." In 2022, the PRC "continued to engage in biological activities with potential BW applications." The United States "does not have sufficient information to determine whether the PRC has eliminated its assessed historical BW program . . . . As part of its historical BW program, the PRC had reportedly weaponized ricin, botulinum toxins, and the causative agents of anthrax, cholera, plague, and tularemia. . . . Retention of latent knowledge and technical capability from the PRC's former undeclared BW program raise concern of the dual-use biological research conducted" by the PRC's People's Liberation Army.
Iran	The United States "continues to assess that Iran has not abandoned its intention to conduct research and development of biological agents and toxins for offensive purposes. . . . Iran maintains flexibility to use, upon leadership demand, legitimate research underway for biodefense and public health purposes for a capability to produce lethal BW agents. . . . Iranian biotechnology entities, particularly military-affiliated institutions, continued to pursue dual-use technologies. Open source reports note Iranian military-associated universities and affiliated research centers have conducted BW-relevant projects on bioregulators."
DPRK	The United States assesses that the DPRK has an offensive BW program and has had BW capabilities since at least the 1960s. The DPRK "probably has the capability to produce sufficient quantities of biological agents for military purposes." The DPRK "probably has the technical capability to produce bacteria, viruses, and toxins that could be used as BW agents." The DPRK "also has at least a limited capability to genetically engineer biological products." "Pyongyang probably is capable of weaponizing BW agents with unconventional systems such as sprayers and poison pen injection devices."
Russia	The United States assesses that "Russia maintains an offensive BW program." "Russia inherited the past offensive program of biological research and development from the Soviet Union. Russia is extensively modernizing Soviet-era biological warfare infrastructure that could support its present-day offensive program."

SOURCE: Features information from DoS, *Adherence to and Compliance with Arms Control, Nonproliferation, and Disarmament Agreements and Commitments*, pp. 23, 24, 26, and 27.

al Qaeda, Aum Shinrikyo, and the Rajneeshee cult—have pursued BW in the past.[13] The Joint Operating Environment 2035 (JOE 2035) document, *The Joint Force in a Contested and Disordered World*, assesses threat trends to inform force development for DoD through 2035,[14] and it states that non-state actors "will eventually obtain chemical, biological, radiological, or even nuclear weapons" by 2035.[15] The JOE 2035 postulates that nonstate actors are more likely to gain chemical, biological, radiological, or nuclear capabilities by "seizure of weapons stockpiles" from state actors who are not, or are not capable of, using proper security measures than by developing such capabilities independently.[16]

International Community Would Face Challenges in Implementing the UNSGM to Investigate and Attribute Alleged BW Use

The UN General Assembly established the UNSGM in 1987 to address international concerns about CW use in the late 1970s and early 1980s, and the UN Security Council reaffirmed the UNSGM-related resolution in 1988.[17] The UNSGM permits the UN secretary-general "to carry out investigations in response to reports that may be brought to his attention by any Member State concerning the possible use of chemical and bacteriological (biological) or toxin weapons that may constitute a violation of the Geneva Protocol or other relevant rules of customary international law to ascertain the facts of the matter and to report promptly the results of any such investigations to all Member States."[18] Implementing the UNSGM to determine the facts, including those related to attribution, regarding alleged BW uses could present sev-

---

[13] Lewis et al., "The Biosecurity Benefits of Genetic Engineering Attribution."

[14] U.S. Joint Chiefs of Staff (JCS), "Joint Operating Environment."

[15] Perkins, "International Mechanisms for the Investigation of Alleged Use of Biological Weapons—A Primer"; JCS, *Joint Operating Environment (JOE) 2035*, p. 9.

[16] JCS, *Joint Operating Environment (JOE) 2035*.

[17] UNODA, "Secretary-General's Mechanism for Investigation of Alleged Use of Chemical and Biological Weapons"; McLeish and Moon, "Sitting on the Boundary."

[18] UNODA, "Fact Sheet: The Secretary-General's Mechanism for Investigation of Alleged Use of Chemical and Biological Weapons, p. 1.

eral challenges—procedural, capability-related, and political, including dis-information campaigns—that the United States and its allies could address to strengthen the UNSGM and reduce risks related to BW use.

Procedural Challenges

The guidelines and procedures for final reports of UNSGM investigations do not specifically address attribution and do not require reports to include an assessment of the actors responsible for alleged BW use:[19]

> In order to conclude the investigation, the team of qualified experts should as early as possible, evaluate all the information available to it, including the results of the laboratory analyses, with a view to pre-paring its final report. The final report prepared by the team for sub-mission to the Secretary-General should include the following: (a) information on the composition of the team at various stages in the investigation, included during the preparation of the report; (b) all rel-evant data gathered during the investigation; (c) a description of the investigation process, tracing the various stages of the investigation with special reference to (i) the locations and time of sampling and in situ analyses, (ii) supporting evidence, such as records of interviews, the results of medical examinations and scientific analyses, documents examined by the team, and (iii) locations and dates of deliberation on the report as well as the date of its adoption, (d) conclusions proposed jointly by the team of qualified experts, indicating the extent to which the alleged events have been substantiated and possibly assessing the probability of their having taken place, (e) individual opinions by member or members of the team of qualified experts dissenting from the majority or differing on any of the points listed above should also be recorded in the report.[20]

Some UN member states might challenge attempts to determine attribu-tion using the UNSGM. However, evidence gathered or considered as part of an UNSGM investigation could implicate the responsible actor(s), even if

---

[19] UNGA Document A/44/561, *Chemical and Bacteriological (Biological) Weapons Report of the Secretary-General*; McLeish and Moon, "Sitting on the Boundary."

[20] UNGA Document A/44/561, *Chemical and Bacteriological (Biological) Weapons Report of the Secretary-General*, p. 30.

the report lacks that explicit assessment. Subsequent investigations by the UN or other entities might determine attribution, as has been the case for investigations of CW use in Syria since 2013.[21]

The Organization for the Prohibition of Chemical Weapons (OPCW)—which is the implementing body for the Chemical Weapons Convention (CWC) and entered into force with the CWC in 1997—is responsible for investigations of CW uses related to its States Parties.[22] The UNSGM, in cooperation with the OPCW and in accordance with the relevant provisions of the CWC treaty, provides for investigations of alleged CW uses related to countries that are not States Parties to the CWC.[23] The OPCW maintains CW experts and laboratory capabilities to assist both States Parties and the UN in investigating alleged CW uses.[24] Since 2013, the OPCW has investigated Russia's use of CW agents in the attempted assassinations of Sergey Skripal in 2018 and Alexey Navalny in 2020 and CW uses in Syria.[25]

The procedures that the international community has used for investigating and attributing CW use in Syria, however, do not serve as a precedent for investigating allegations of BW use. The Biological and Toxins Weapons Convention (BWC), which entered into force in 1975, does not have an implementing body like the OPCW, and, as mentioned previously, the UNSGM is the only international mechanism for investigating alleged

---

[21] Koblentz, "Chemical-Weapon Use in Syria Atrocities, Attribution, and Accountability"; Arms Control Association, "Timeline of Syrian Chemical Weapons Activity, 2012–2022"; Chevrier, "Compliance Mechanisms and Their Implementation."

[22] According to Article I of the CWC treaty, States Parties agree not

> [t]o develop, produce, otherwise acquire, stockpile or retain chemical weapons, or transfer, directly or indirectly, chemical weapons to anyone; to use chemical weapons; to engage in any military preparations to use chemical weapons; or to assist, encourage or induce, in any way, anyone to engage in any activity prohibited to a State Party [under the CWC]. (Convention on the Prohibition of the Development, Production, Stockpiling and Use of Chemical Weapons and on their Destruction [CWC]).

[23] UNODA, "Secretary-General's Mechanism for Investigation of Alleged Use of Chemical and Biological Weapons"; UNGA Document A/44/561, *Chemical and Bacteriological (Biological) Weapons Report of the Secretary-General.*

[24] OPCW, "Responding to the Use of Chemical Weapons."

[25] OPCW, "Incident in Salisbury"; OPCW, "OPCW Provides Technical Assistance to Germany Regarding Allegations of Chemical Weapons Use Against Alexei Navalny."

BW use.[26] According to Article I of the BWC, States Parties to the BWC treaty agree not to "develop, produce, stockpile, or otherwise acquire or retain: microbial or other biological agents, or toxins whatever their origin or method of production, of types and in quantities that have no justification for prophylactic, protective or other peaceful purposes;" and "weapons, equipment or means of delivery designed to use such agents or toxins for hostile purposes or in armed conflict." Article VI of the BWC allows for State Parties to "lodge a complaint" with the UN Security Council if they find "any other State Party is acting in breach of obligations deriving from the provisions" of the BWC, which UNODA states includes BW use.[27] Article VI also calls on each State Party to cooperate in any investigations that the Security Council might initiate to address the complaint.[28] The implementation procedures to trigger a UNSGM investigation of alleged BW use through the BWC's Article VI are less developed than the international processes for investigating alleged CW use because the international community implemented and strengthened CW-related processes—through the UN and the OPCW—to respond to CW use in Syria.[29]

Capability-Related Challenges

To enable successful attribution, investigations of biological incidents should begin as soon as a potential incident is detected.[30] Many countries do not have the capabilities or expertise necessary to launch an investigation quickly, and they most likely will turn to the UN Security Council to

---

[26] UNODA, "Secretary-General's Mechanism for Investigation of Alleged Use of Chemical and Biological Weapons"; UNODA, "The Fact Sheet: Secretary-General's Mechanism for Investigation of Alleged Use of Chemical and Biological Weapons"; Switzerland Federal Department of Defense Spiez Laboratory, *UNSGM Designated Laboratories Workshop Report.*

[27] UNODA, "Fact Sheet: The Secretary-General's Mechanism for Investigation of Alleged Use of Chemical and Biological Weapons."

[28] Convention on the Prohibition of the Development, Production and Stockpiling of Bacteriological (Biological) and Toxin Weapons and On Their Destruction (BWC), Art. I.

[29] Green, "The Mechanisms Behind the United Nations Secretary-General's Mechanism."

[30] de Bretton-Gordon, "Biosecurity in the Wake of COVID-19."

do so.[31] The OPCW's efforts to investigate and attribute CW use in Syria highlighted the importance of a central repository of CW experts and analytical laboratories to provide technical support.[32] The BWC has no implementing body to maintain similar vital resources. UNODA, which the UN established in 1998, is the custodian of the UNSGM and has the task of ensuring that the UN is prepared to conduct investigations as requested by member states. In 2007, UNODA organized a group of experts to update the UNSGM's guidelines and procedures, which were initially established in 1989. The group prepared updates with particular consideration for technical aspects of investigations of alleged BW use.[33] Since 2007, UNODA has been working with member states to establish and maintain cadres of BW experts and analytical laboratories, and it coordinates related training activities with member states, laboratories, and international organizations. If the UNSGM is activated, the UN secretary-general can request assistance from this cadre of BW experts and laboratories on short notice and can also request support and expertise from the OPCW, the World Health Organization, and the World Organization for Animal Health.[34]

Political Challenges

The OPCW has built international credibility through its multiple investigations of CW use,[35] but the UN has yet to demonstrate its capabilities related to UNSGM investigations of alleged BW use. Some member states might use this inexperience to question the expertise and technical capabilities of the UN's cadre of BW experts and analytical laboratories, and

---

[31] de Bretton-Gordon, "Biosecurity in the Wake of COVID-19."

[32] Chevrier, "Compliance Mechanisms and Their Implementation."

[33] UNODA, "Fact Sheet: The Secretary-General's Mechanism for Investigation of Alleged Use of Chemical and Biological Weapons."

[34] UNODA, "Secretary-General's Mechanism for Investigation of Alleged Use of Chemical and Biological Weapons"; UNODA, "The Fact Sheet: Secretary-General's Mechanism for Investigation of Alleged Use of Chemical and Biological Weapons"; Chevrier, "Compliance Mechanisms and Their Implementation"; Switzerland Federal Department of Defense Spiez Laboratory, *UNSGM Designated Laboratories Workshop Report.*

[35] Chevrier, "Compliance Mechanisms and Their Implementation."

UNODA is trying to expand and diversify the cadre to strengthen the group's credibility.[36]

Some member states might also choose to accuse the United States and its allies of politicizing the UNSGM, especially if the United States is directly involved in requests for or support of investigations. U.S. adversaries could also wage disinformation campaigns to discredit UNSGM investigations of alleged BW use and their conclusions, especially if UNSGM reports include attribution assessments. Syria and Russia consistently denied Syria's culpability and objected to OPCW reports that attributed responsibility of CW use in Syria to the Syrian government.[37] In October 2022, Russia lodged a formal complaint to the UN Security Council under Article VI of the BWC with accusations that the United States and Ukraine had not provided necessary explanations about the operation of biological laboratories in Ukraine.[38] Prior to its formal complaint, Russia had spread the public narrative that the United States was funding a network of BW laboratories in Ukraine.[39] The UN Security Council did not approve Russia's resolution to invoke Article VI,[40] but this episode demonstrates Russia's willingness to spread disinformation and misuse international organizations for its own political gains.

---

[36] UNODA, "Fact Sheet: The Secretary-General's Mechanism for Investigation of Alleged Use of Chemical and Biological Weapons."

[37] Becker-Jakob, "Countering the Use of Chemical Weapons in Syria: Options for Supporting International Norms and Institutions"; Leitenberg, "False Allegations of Biological-Weapons Use from Putin's Russia."

[38] UN, "UN Still Sees No Sign of Biological Weapons in Ukraine."

[39] Quinn, "Russia Calls Meeting of Biological Weapons Convention."

[40] UN, "UN/Ukraine Biological Weapons."

Research Questions

In this report, we address how DoD can lead and contribute to the U.S. government's efforts to strengthen the UNSGM to determine the facts, including those related to attribution, regarding the alleged use of BW or toxin weapons. We do so by assessing the following questions:

- Why is attribution of BW use important?
- During a biological incident, including BW use, what evidence might provide valuable information to facilitate attribution?
- What is the state of the science for determining the origin of a biological incident, including BW use?
- What capabilities does DoD possess or could it develop to facilitate attribution of BW use?

Findings

Attribution Is Difficult but Essential to Support International Efforts to Counter BW

Determining attribution can be difficult, but developing and maintaining robust capabilities and processes to conduct investigations of alleged BW use and determine the actor(s) responsible are an important part of reinforcing international norms against BW use. Information from investigations of alleged BW use can (1) help develop a better understanding of adversaries' BW-related capabilities and doctrine, (2) inform improvements to biodefense capabilities, (3) provide evidence to support international responses to BW use and help hold perpetrators accountable, and (4) act as a deterrent to future BW use or development.

Determining the source of a biological incident—whether natural, accidental, or deliberate—is difficult for many reasons. BW agents can cause diseases that also occur naturally, and differentiating between natural and deliberate biological incidents can be difficult for this reason. Collecting, analyzing, and interpreting technical information about a pathogen that causes a biological incident could be complicated by lack of access to the affected area or victims or to technology or genomic data that can provide the exact technical characteristics of the pathogen. People may not recognize when they are exposed to pathogens that cause diseases, and symptoms of exposure can be delayed, further complicating determination of the source.[41]

The IC's attempts to ascertain the origin of the COVID-19 pandemic illustrates the difficulty in determining the cause of biological incidents. In a June 2023 report, the IC presents the IC agencies' differing assessments on COVID-19 origins.[42] According to this report, all IC agencies "continue to assess that both a natural and laboratory-associated origin remain plausible hypotheses to explain the first human infection" with SARS-CoV-2, the virus that causes COVID-19, and that "SARS-CoV-2 was not developed as a BW agent."[43] However, IC agencies remain split on which of the two plausible hypotheses is the most likely, even though the agencies have been analyzing related information, some of which is not publicly available, since the COVID-19 pandemic started in 2020. The Department of Energy and the FBI both assess "that a laboratory-associated incident was the most likely cause of the first human infection," but they come to this conclusion for different reasons.[44] The Central Intelligence Agency and one other IC agency "remain unable to determine the precise origin of the COVID-19 pandemic," and they do not make an assessment on the cause of the first human infection.[45]

---

[41] Johansson, "Towards a UNSGM Biological Analysis Network"; McLeish and Moon, "Sitting on the Boundary."

[42] ODNI, *Potential Links Between the Wuhan Institute of Virology and the Origin of the COVID-19 Pandemic*.

[43] ODNI, *Potential Links Between the Wuhan Institute of Virology and the Origin of the COVID-19 Pandemic*, p. 3.

[44] ODNI, *Potential Links Between the Wuhan Institute of Virology and the Origin of the COVID-19 Pandemic*, p. 3.

[45] ODNI, *Potential Links Between the Wuhan Institute of Virology and the Origin of the COVID-19 Pandemic*; McLeish and Moon, "Sitting on the Boundary."

Despite the difficulty, investigations of alleged BW uses are important because the evidence collected can improve the understanding of BW threats, strengthen international awareness of BW risks, and inform efforts to mitigate harm from BW uses. Strengthening worldwide capabilities to investigate alleged BW uses would make a significant contribution to deterring use because adversaries would be less able to hide their BW-related activities.[46] Investigations of alleged BW use provide insights into adversaries' BW capabilities and doctrines, leading to a more complete understanding of BW-related threats to national security. Properly investigating and attributing alleged BW use also informs development of methods to detect, deter, and disrupt BW programs and uses. Understanding all aspects of a BW use allows development of measures to prevent, prepare for, and recover from future BW uses.[47]

The United States, its allies, and other nations do not develop BW capabilities, consider BW development and use to be unacceptable, and seek to hold accountable those actors who use BW.[48] Confident identification of actors who use BW is required to enable the international community to levy appropriate and effective consequences for BW use.[49] Taking action against those who use BW demonstrates that such behavior has a cost, providing deterrence to further use. Demonstrating capabilities to attribute BW use serves as a deterrent against state and nonstate actors who are considering conducting a BW attack or developing BW capabilities because it increases the possibility that they will be identified and punished.[50]

---

[46] McLeish and Moon, "Sitting on the Boundary."

[47] Lewis et al., "The Biosecurity Benefits of Genetic Engineering Attribution."

[48] OPCW Executive Council EC-96/NAT.24, *United States of America: Statement by H.E. Ambassador Joseph Manso Permanent Representative of the United States of America to the OPCW at the Ninety-Sixth Session of the Executive Council*; OPCW Executive Council EC-102/NAT.9, *United States of America: Statement by H.E. Ambassador Joseph Manso Permanent Representative of the United States of America at the OPCW at the 102nd Session of the Executive Council.*

[49] UNGA Document GA/DIS/3666, "Use of Chemical, Biological Weapons Unacceptable in Any Context, Delegates Stress, as First Committee Continues General Debate."

[50] Lewis et al., "The Biosecurity Benefits of Genetic Engineering Attribution"; OPCW, *Note by the Technical Secretariat: The OPCW in 2025: Ensuring a World Free of Chemical Weapons.*

Attribution Assessments Are Strengthened by a Variety of Evidence from a Biological Incident

Investigators can draw more confident attribution conclusions when they have more high-quality information from a variety of sources that provides insights to different aspects of a biological incident. Figure 1 provides a notional timeline of a biological incident and, for each stage, lists evidence that could inform attribution assessments and opportunities for collecting such evidence. IC agencies might collect information prior to a biological incident that could be valuable to attribution assessments of BW uses, even when the information does not provide warning of imminent use. Investigators and analysts could use such intelligence reporting with other information gained from investigations during and in the immediate aftermath of a biological incident to provide a more complete understanding of what occurred, how it occurred, and who or what was responsible. For example, analysis of physiological and environmental samples from a biological incident could reveal characteristics of the causative biological agent that intelligence reporting indicates are unique to unnatural biological agents or production methods that a certain actor uses. These two sources of information by themselves might not be sufficient to identify the perpetrator with any confidence, but, together, they allow investigators and analysts to draw conclusions with more certainty.

Investigations of biological incidents could benefit from lessons learned during international efforts since 2013 to examine and attribute allegations of CW use in Syria.[51] In Appendix 2 of its final report from December

---

[51] UNGA Security Council Document A/67/997-S/2013/553, *Report of the United Nations Mission to Investigate Allegations of the Use of Chemical Weapons in the Syrian Arab Republic on the Alleged Use of Chemical Weapons in the Ghouta Area of Damascus on 21 August 2013*; UNGA Security Council Document A/68/663-S/2013/735, *Identical Letters Dated 13 December 2013 from the Secretary-General Addressed to the President of the General Assembly and the President of the Security Council*; OPCW, *Note by the Technical Secretariat: First Report by the OPCW Investigation and Identification Team Pursuant to Paragraph 10 of Decision C-SS-4/Dec.3 'Addressing the Threat From Chemical Weapons Use' Ltamenah (Syrian Arab Republic) 24, 25, and 30 March 2017*; OPCW, *Note by the Technical Secretariat: Second Report by the OPCW Investigation and Identification Team Pursuant to Paragraph 10 of Decision C-SS-4/Dec.3 'Addressing the Threat From Chemical Weapons Use' Saraqib (Syrian Arab Republic)–4 February 2018*;

FIGURE 1

Notional Timeline of a Biological Incident Illustrating Possible Evidence of Interest During Different Stages of the Incident

	Possible evidence	Evidence collection opportunities
Pre-incident	• Intelligence reporting of plans for BW use and adversaries' BW capabilities and doctrine for use • Adversaries' narratives in traditional media reporting or social media postings	• Monitor traditional news outlets and social media for indications that a biological incident is occurring or has occurred • Collect and analyze data from biosurveillance systems • Collect intelligence from assessed BW-related entities
Incident	• Biosurveillance data analysis • Reports from hospitals about increased admittance and victims' symptoms • Social media postings or media reporting about an attack or about victims experiencing symptoms • Location and identities of aircraft, troops, or other military components in the area • Characteristics of the incident	• Monitor status and medical treatment of victims • Collect physiological and environmental samples • Collect intelligence incident information from all possible sources
Immediate aftermath and response	• Fragments of munitions or other delivery methods • Results from analysis of physiological and environmental samples	• Monitor adversaries' responses, including public narratives • Analyze physiological and environmental samples
Recovery	• Biosurveillance data analysis • Adversaries' responses to political, economic, or military actions to hold actors accountable for BW use	• Monitor adversaries' responses to actions to hold actors accountable for BW use • Conduct analysis of lessons learned and related capabilities gaps • Reconsider assessments of perpetrators' BW capabilities

SOURCE: Features information from Katz et al., "Mapping Stakeholders and Policies in Response to Deliberate Biological Events."

and OPCW, *Note by the Technical Secretariat, Third Report by the OPCW Investigation*

2013, the UN documented its methodology, including the types of evidence collected: "bio-medical samples, environmental samples, witness interviews/statements (collected as audio and video) and documents, photos and videos."[52] The UN mission's "methods for interviews, sampling, and documentation" followed "well established standard operating procedures (SOPs), developed and enforced by the OPCW and the [World Health Organization] WHO."[53] The OPCW's documents contain guidelines and best practices—including those related to collecting and handling evidence, training personnel, and analyzing evidence—that could apply to or be adapted for investigation of biological incidents.[54]

Evidence Could Help Distinguish Natural or Accidental Biological Incidents from Deliberate Ones

The first indicators that a biological incident—whether natural, accidental, or deliberate— has occurred might include reports, possibly on social media or from hospitals, of clusters of victims experiencing similar symptoms. In the case of BW use, indicators could include either intelligence reports warning of an imminent BW attack or overt signs of an attack, such as munitions or other devices used to deliver the BW agent. BW attacks could, however, be covert and lack such indicators, complicating or delaying efforts to distinguish between natural, accidental, and deliberate biological incidents.

---

and Identification Team Pursuant to Paragraph 10 of Decision C-SS-4/Dec.3 'Addressing the Threat From Chemical Weapons Use' Douma (Syrian Arab Republic)–7 April 2018.

[52] UNGA Security Council Document A/67/997-S/2013/553, *Report of the United Nations Mission to Investigate Allegations of the Use of Chemical Weapons in the Syrian Arab Republic on the Alleged Use of Chemical Weapons in the Ghouta Area of Damascus on 21 August 2013*, p. 11/41; McLeish and Moon, "Sitting on the Boundary."

[53] UNGA Security Council Document A/67/997-S/2013/553, *Report of the United Nations Mission to Investigate Allegations of the Use of Chemical Weapons in the Syrian Arab Republic on the Alleged Use of Chemical Weapons in the Ghouta Area of Damascus on 21 August 2013*, p. 5/41.

[54] UNGA Security Council Document A/67/997-S/2013/553, *Report of the United Nations Mission to Investigate Allegations of the Use of Chemical Weapons in the Syrian Arab Republic on the Alleged Use of Chemical Weapons in the Ghouta Area of Damascus on 21 August 2013*; McLeish and Moon, "Sitting on the Boundary."

Determining the cause of a biological incident is complicated because, as mentioned previously, some biological agents have natural, common sources and can cause natural or accidental outbreaks of disease.[55] For that reason, natural, accidental, and deliberate biological incidents can display similar characteristics and, especially in the absence of other information, investigations of deliberate biological incidents as crimes can be delayed. For example, in 1984, public health officials in The Dalles, Oregon, initially thought that an outbreak of *Salmonella* infections was more likely to be natural or accidental than deliberate, despite documentation in the country of at least 751 cases during the outbreak. Prior to this outbreak, the county had usually reported less than five cases of *Salmonella* infections per year. Dismissal of this indicator delayed proper attribution until about a year later when the FBI found evidence tying the Rajneesh religious community to that outbreak. The FBI found in the Rajneesh compound a vial of *S. Typhimurium*—one of the causative agents of *Salmonella* infections—that was the same strain as the one that caused the outbreak in 1984. Leaders in the Rajneesh movement eventually admitted to contaminating a city water supply tank with *S. Typhimurium* to cause a deliberate Salmonella outbreak and affect county elections.[56] Looking for indicators early in an investigation that a biological incident is deliberate can help justify further examination, which facilitates faster attribution. Table 2 lists key indicators that can signal that a biological incident is deliberate rather than natural or accidental. If one or more of these indicators are observed during a biological incident, an investigation should begin immediately. The investigation may conclude that the biological incident is accidental or natural, but an early investigation would help strengthen attribution in cases of deliberate BW uses.

---

[55] United Nations Interregional Crime and Justice Research Institute (UNICRI), *A Prosecutor's Guide to Chemical and Biological Crimes*.

[56] McDade, Joseph, and David Franz, "Bioterrorism as a Public Health Threat"; Naval Postgraduate School Center for Homeland Defense and Security, "Timeline—Rajneeshee Bioterror Attack"; Clark, "Bioterrorism Beginnings."

TABLE 2

Key Indicators That a Biological Incident Is Deliberate

	Indicators
1	Case(s) of disease caused by an unusual biological agent (e.g., eradicated agent, novel agent, unusual agent strain)
2	Epidemiological inconsistency (e.g., unusual disease presentation, unusual geographic presentation, unusual seasonal distribution, unusual number of infected individuals, high number of infections in a disparate population, unusual host range, multiple strains emerging at the same time)
3	Higher morbidity or mortality than expected for the type of biological agent
4	Unusual characteristics of the biological agent (e.g., higher pathogenicity, greater transmissibility, lower susceptibility to medical countermeasures)
5	Unusual disease in animal population (e.g., unusual number of animal illnesses or deaths)
6	Unusual disease in agriculture (e.g., unusual number of crops die off)
7	Laboratory breach (e.g., missing biological agents, missing equipment, cyberattack)
8	Existence of credible threat (e.g., whistleblower, reported suspicious behavior, online monitoring)
9	Time and location of the incident coincide with a special date or location (e.g., near key assets, on an important anniversary)

Proper Collection, Handling, Analysis, and Reporting of Evidence Facilitate Attribution

The quality of an attribution assessment of a deliberate biological incident depends on the quality of the information on which it is based. The source, handling, and transfer of evidence can affect the related interpretation and analysis and the quality of the reported results. Physiological and environmental samples should be collected and handled using methods that avoid contamination, preserve sample integrity, and maintain chain of custody. Interviews should be conducted to avoid misinterpretation and inaccurate reporting of statements from victims, witnesses, and others involved in the incident. Investigation teams should try to confirm the source and validity of evidence that representatives from governments or other organizations contribute to the investigation. These considerations are all aimed at building the best possible support for attribution assessments and ensuring that they can withstand challenges from those who might seek to undermine them for political or other reasons. Investigation teams should be trained on proper collection, handling, analysis, and reporting of evidence and should have the necessary equipment to do so. Other support teams, such as first responders and recovery groups, should also be aware of these issues to preserve opportunities to collect evidence, including samples, in the immediate response and recovery stages of a biological incident.[57]

Investigators should attempt to collect samples—including physiological samples, environmental samples, and remains of any munitions or other delivery devices—from a variety of sources—including exposed humans, animals, soil, and water—to allow for corroboration of results and to strengthen analytical results. Collection of control, baseline, or background samples—that were not exposed to the biological agent but are representative of the relevant population or environment—provides reference points for comparison with exposed samples. This comparison helps determine whether the amount of biological agents identified in exposed samples is significant relative to endemic levels and natural or expected levels in the human or animal bodies or the local environment. Biological agents can undergo different processes for distribution and metabolization within human and animal bodies. Collecting a variety of physiological samples— including blood, urine, and hair—decreases the risk that an agent will be present in the body but not detected in collected physiological samples. If possible, trained medical professionals should collect physiological samples under the investigation team's supervision.[58]

---

[57] Switzerland Federal Department of Defense Spiez Laboratory, *UNSGM Designated Laboratories Workshop Report*; UNGA Security Council Document A/67/997-S/2013/553, *Report of the United Nations Mission to Investigate Allegations of the Use of Chemical Weapons in the Syrian Arab Republic on the Alleged Use of Chemical Weapons in the Ghouta Area of Damascus on 21 August 2013*.

[58] Green, "The Mechanisms Behind the United Nations Secretary-General's Mechanism"; UNGA Security Council Document A/67/997-S/2013/553, *Report of the United Nations Mission to Investigate Allegations of the Use of Chemical Weapons in the Syrian Arab Republic on the Alleged Use of Chemical Weapons in the Ghouta Area of Damascus on 21 August 2013*; Switzerland Federal Department of Defense Spiez Laboratory, *UNSGM Designated Laboratories Workshop Report*.

To collect any samples, the investigative team will require access to the exposed victims and the location of the biological incident. The UNSGM requires member states to cooperate with investigations, which would include allowing investigation teams access to locations of alleged BW uses, but inspectors should plan to be flexible and adapt if they are denied access.[59] Organizations that might be involved in sample collection and analysis should, before a biological incident occurs, establish processes for moving samples from the location of collection to laboratories for analysis. UNODA maintains a list of analytical laboratories, which included 88 facilities from 30 member states in 2020.[60] Maintaining and documenting the chain of custody for samples related to biological incidents are important to protect the integrity of the samples and strengthen any assessments based on the analysis of the samples. Such processes should consider and adhere to regulations related to transporting living organisms and other sample types across international boundaries.[61]

In addition to samples, trained inspectors should interview victims, witnesses, first responders, medical staff, and suspected actors involved in BW use. Investigative teams should document information from doctors and other medical officials about symptoms, changes in medical status, laboratory analysis, and medical treatment related to victims of biological incidents.[62] Investigation teams should also document interviews using audio or video recordings to allow for thorough review and analysis and to pre-

---

[59] Convention on the Prohibition of the Development, Production and Stockpiling of Bacteriological (Biological) and Toxin Weapons and On Their Destruction (BWC).

[60] UNODA, "Fact Sheet: The Secretary-General's Mechanism for Investigation of Alleged Use of Chemical and Biological Weapons." In the United States, facilities within the Laboratory Response Network for Biological Threats respond to and receive samples from deliberate biological incidents.

[61] Switzerland Federal Department of Defense Spiez Laboratory, *UNSGM Designated Laboratories Workshop Report.*

[62] Green, "The Mechanisms Behind the United Nations Secretary-General's Mechanism."

vent errors in interpretation that could result from incomplete or incorrect notetaking or recollection.[63]

A Range of Technical Capabilities Is Needed to Facilitate Attribution

To first identify that a biological incident occurred and then determine the origin or establish attribution requires a range of technical capabilities. Various national and international biosurveillance systems are in place to monitor for biological agents and to report in real time whether a biological incident has occurred. Technical capabilities are needed to collect, package, and transport samples properly, especially because samples related to biological incidents can contain high-risk pathogens. Laboratory personnel need technologies to analyze physiological, environmental, and other samples sufficiently to identify characteristics that could help identify the biological agent's origin.[64]

A microbial forensic investigation usually includes identifying and characterizing the causative biological agent and detecting anomalies in the epidemiological development of the related disease or illness.[65] Investigative teams can use two key biotechnology areas to aid in determining BW use attribution: biosurveillance technology and microbial forensics technology. Biosurveillance technology and systems monitor for biological incidents and alert the authorities responsible for responding when one is detected.[66] For example, one system that uses biosurveillance technology is the DoD-Global Emerging Infections Surveillance Electronic Surveillance System for the Early Notification of Community-Based Epidemics (ESSENCE), which

---

[63] UNGA Security Council Document A/67/997-S/2013/553, *Report of the United Nations Mission to Investigate Allegations of the Use of Chemical Weapons in the Syrian Arab Republic on the Alleged Use of Chemical Weapons in the Ghouta Area of Damascus on 21 August 2013.*

[64] UNICRI, *A Prosecutor's Guide to Chemical and Biological Crimes.*

[65] Johansson, "Towards a UNSGM Biological Analysis Network."

[66] Moore, Fisher, and Stevens, *Toward Integrated DoD Biosurveillance: Assessment and Opportunities.*

could provide early warning of disease anomalies. The ESSENCE system monitors DoD outpatient health care data from around the world for certain medical issues and trends of public health interest using detection methods developed in partnership with Johns Hopkins University. The system allows Defense Health Agency epidemiologists and public health officers to obtain medical situational awareness and investigate reportable disease events.[67]

Microbial forensics involves using epidemiology and microbiologic technology to characterize biological agents and identify their origins, whether natural or synthetic.[68] Table 3 provides a list of several key technologies used in microbial forensics. These technologies not only help identify and characterize the biological agent but also help determine potential human manipulation or weaponization and possible dissemination methodology. Such information could result in stronger attribution assessments.[69]

Attribution of BW uses probably will require technical capabilities to identify a variety of biological agents, including novel ones that are not included in the U.S. government's Federal Select Agent Program or the Australia Group List of Human and Animal Pathogens and Toxins for Export Control. These lists serve as references for U.S. and international efforts to prevent biological incidences by identifying biological agents and toxins that pose significant threats to human, animal, or plant health.[70] The United States and the international community have focused primarily on these lists when establishing export controls and defensive countermeasures, including detectors, and adversaries might seek to develop agents not included on these lists to evade such measures. For example, in the attempted assas-

[67] Military Health System and Defense Health Agency, "Electronic Surveillance System for the Early Notification of Community-Based Epidemics."

[68] Khan, Amara, and Morse, "Forensic Public Health: Epidemiological and Microbiological Investigations for Biosecurity."

[69] UNICRI, *A Prosecutor's Guide to Chemical and Biological Crimes.*

[70] Centers for Disease Control and Prevention (CDC), U.S. Department of Human and Health Services (HHS), and U.S. Department of Agriculture (USDA), "Federal Select Agent Program"; The Australia Group (AG), "List of Human and Animal Pathogens and Toxins for Export Control."

TABLE 3

Key Microbial Forensics Technologies

Technology	Notes
Lateral flow assays (LFA)	• Laboratory testing: rapidly detects the presence of a specific biological agent • Can provide results in less than two hours • Can provide presumptive positive • In-field testing possible, can provide indicative positive
Enzyme-linked immunosorbent assay (ELISA)	• Laboratory testing: detects the presence of a specific biological agent • Can provide results in less than two hours • Can provide presumptive positive • In-field testing possible, can provide indicative positive
Polymerase chain reaction (PCR)	• Laboratory testing: detects the presence of a specific organism • Can provide results in half a day to days • Can provide presumptive positive
Liquid chromatography-mass spectrometry (LC-MS) and liquid chromatography with high resolution mass spectrometer (LC-HRMS)	• Laboratory testing: chemically analyzes and characterizes a sample • Can provide results in more than half a day to months • Can provide unambiguous positive
DNA sequencing	• Laboratory procedure: decodes a biological agent's genetic material • Can provide results in more than a day to months • Can provide the exact sequence of nucleotides of a sample

SOURCE: OPCW, *Analysis of Biotoxins*; Knobler, Mahmoud, and Pray, *Biological Threat and Terrorism*; Alhajj, Zuhair, and Farhana, "Enzyme Linked Immunosorbent Assay"; Persons, *Science and Tech Spotlight*.

NOTE: This is not an exhaustive list, but it does highlight some technologies that exist and that investigative teams could use to aid in identifying and characterizing biological agents. An indicative positive test result indicates that the agent may be present but requires more-sophisticated testing to confirm the presence of the agent. A presumptive positive test result signals the presence of an agent but still requires official confirmation by more rigorous laboratory testing and analysis by a public health agency, usually at the federal or state level. An unambiguous positive test result provides complete certainty about the presence and characteristics of the agent but could still require official confirmation by a public health agency at the federal or state level. As a precaution, any positive result is treated as a positive until officially confirmed.

sinations of Skripal and Navalny, Russia used two CW agents that are not included in the CWC treaty's Annex on Chemicals.[71]

Some emerging technology advancements in the microbial forensic field could enhance BW investigation capabilities, especially for novel or manipulated agents. For example, next-generation sequencing technology enables the rapid characterization of pathogens, making it easier to track and identify a pathogen's origins.[72] Metagenomics technology enables DNA sequencing extracted directly from environmental samples, which can assist in identifying specific pathogens in a complex ecosystem. The ability of bioinformatic tools to handle vast amounts of biological data allows for quick and accurate analysis of genomic data.[73] Machine learning and artificial intelligence models help analyze and interpret complex datasets and identify or make predictions about potential biological threats.[74] Other technological advancements and trends include CRISPR-based technologies adapted for diagnostic purposes, lab-on-a-chip miniaturized analytical devices for rapid pathogen detection out in the field, and single-cell RNA sequencing technologies for identifying complex cell populations within complex microbial communities.[75]

These and future advancements can provide opportunities for investigators to determine the origin of an agent effectively and rapidly during an intentional biological incident. Therefore, continued investment in these technologies is critical to maintaining and growing these capabilities for investigators. Stopping or minimizing investments could lead to an erosion in these capabilities, potentially allowing adversaries an advantage. Devel-

---

[71] OPCW, "Incident in Salisbury"; OPCW, "OPCW Provides Technical Assistance to Germany Regarding Allegations of Chemical Weapons Use Against Alexei Navalny."

[72] Gwinn, MacCannell, and Armstrong, "Next-Generation Sequencing of Infectious Pathogens."

[73] Roumpeka et al., "A Review of Bioinformatics Tools for Bio-Prospecting from Metagenomic Sequence Data."

[74] Ghannam and Techtmann, "Machine Learning Applications in Microbial Ecology, Human Microbiome Studies, and Environmental Monitoring."

[75] Puig-Serra et al., "CRISPR Approaches for the Diagnosis of Human Diseases"; Ghoorchian et al., "Chapter 11–Lab-on-a-Chip Miniaturized Analytical Devices"; Jovic et al., "Single-Cell RNA Sequencing Technologies and Applications: A Brief Overview."

oping effective policies related to these technology areas is also important for supporting legitimate development of these technologies while safeguarding against misuse.

Recommendations for DoD

Using the research presented in the previous sections, we submit the following areas in which DoD could enhance its capabilities to support U.S. efforts to investigate alleged BW uses and, thus, strengthen the UNSGM. Further research and analysis could help prioritize which areas would be most beneficial for DoD to concentrate its efforts and could help identify specific actions DoD could take to make progress in these areas.

Enhance and Build Flexibility and Redundancy, as Appropriate, into DoD's Processes and Capabilities to Investigate and Attribute of Biological Incidents

- Enhance DoD's capabilities globally, as appropriate, to collect information, including intelligence before and after biological incidents, and samples related to biological incidents.
- Continue to work with allies to build their capabilities to collect information and samples related to biological incidents, especially those that occur in locations where DoD has fewer allies or less access.
- Continue to build DoD's capabilities to analyze samples related to biological incidents and work with allies to build their capabilities.
- Exercise and update processes to conduct sampling-related activities, including collecting samples, handling and transporting samples, communicating and collaborating with other U.S. government departments and agencies, protecting patient information, communicating and collaborating with allies, analyzing samples, and reporting and sharing results of sample analysis.
- Improve and exercise procedures to maintain and document chain of custody for samples collected from biological incidents.

- Exercise and update processes to collect intelligence information, including interviewing victims, witnesses, and medical personnel.
- Enhance efforts to train U.S. personnel and partners on methodologies to collect and analyze evidence during investigations of alleged BW use and on processes to share and report results.

Continue to Invest in Biotechnology, Including Microbial Forensic Technology.

- Develop, improve, and refine methods to analyze a broader scope of biological agents than those contained in the Federal Select Agent Program or in the Australia Group List of Human and Animal Pathogens and Toxins for Export Control.[76]
- Develop, improve, and refine capabilities to model biological incidents.
- Consider investing in field-deployable technology or ways of quickly transporting such analytical capabilities to the field to facilitate rapid response to biological incidents.
- Continue efforts to provide training and help develop technical capabilities of UNSGM-designated laboratories.

Maintain Transparency About DoD Efforts to Work with International Partners on Biosecurity and Biodefense Efforts.

- Continue countering false narratives that DoD is supporting offensive BW-related work worldwide.
- Continue and strengthen messaging campaigns, as appropriate, prior to cooperating with international partners on biosecurity and biodefense efforts. Carefully consider how cooperative biosecurity and biodefense efforts could appear to the general public and consider preempting and decreasing the effectiveness of adversaries' related disinformation campaigns.

---

[76] CDC, HHS, and USDA, "Federal Select Agent Program"; The Australia Group, "List of Human and Animal Pathogens and Toxins for Export Control."

NBS Actions for Which DoD has a Lead Role

We present, for reference, NBS actions for which DoD has lead roles but that are outside the scope of this study. DoD was also tasked with various supporting efforts.[77] Table A.1 highlights both assigned lead and supporting efforts for DoD. We include here only the goals, priorities, targets, and actions for which the NBS assigned roles to DoD.

NBS Goal 2. Ensure Biodefense Enterprise Capabilities to Prevent Bioincidents

"The United States will work to prevent the outbreak and spread of naturally occurring infectious diseases and minimize the risk of laboratory accidents both domestically and globally. The United States will also strengthen biosecurity to prevent both state and nonstate actors from obtaining or using biological material, equipment, and expertise for nefarious purposes, consistent with the U.S. Government's approach to countering weapons of mass destruction."

---

[77] In this appendix, unless otherwise indicated, all of the quoted text is directly from White House, *National Biodefense Strategy and Implementation Plan for Countering Biological Threats, Enhancing Pandemic Preparedness, and Achieving Global Health Security*, pp. vii, viii, ix, xi, xii.

Priority 2.2. Prevention

"Prevent nationally or internationally significant biological incidents by (a) minimizing the chances of laboratory accidents; (b) reducing the likelihood of deliberate use or accidental misuse; (c) ensuring effective biosafety and biosecurity practices and oversight; (d) promoting responsible research and innovation; and (e) reducing the likelihood of animal to human spillover of zoonotic pathogens."

Target 2.2.4. Deter Biological Weapons

"Strengthen (1) the international norms against biological weapons (BW) and (2) the mechanisms and tools needed to hold state and nonstate actors accountable for BW development, proliferation, use, or the deliberate misuse of biological research, technologies, and knowledge." Specifically, DoD is tasked with leading the following actions:

I. "Work with foreign partners to strengthen the international security communities' capabilities to recognize, interdict, disable, and destroy biological weapons and weapons-related equipment, material, means of delivery, and facilities, as well as to attribute responsibility for their use. (Lead: DOS, **DoD**; Support: DHS [Department of Homeland Security], FBI)"

II. "Strengthen the implementation of the Biological Weapons Convention and United Nations Security Council Resolution 1540 in order to prevent nation-state or nonstate development, acquisition, or use of biological weapons, related materials, or means of delivery. (Lead: DOS, **DoD**; Support: DOT [Department of Transportation], DOE [Department of Energy], FBI)"

III. "Strengthen the capability of the UN Secretary-General's Mechanism for Investigation of Alleged Use of Chemical and Biological Weapons (UNSGM) to determine the facts, including attribution, regarding the alleged use of biological or toxin weapons. (Lead: DOS, **DoD**, FBI)"

NBS Goal 3. Ensure Biodefense Enterprise Preparedness to Reduce the Impacts of Bioincidents

"The United States will take measures to reduce the impacts of bioincidents, including maintaining a vibrant national science and technology base to support biodefense; promoting a strong domestic and international public, veterinary, and plant health infrastructure; developing, updating, and exercising response and recovery capabilities; establishing risk communications; developing and effectively distributing and dispensing countermeasures; and collaborating across the country and internationally to support biodefense."

Priority 3.1. Domestic Health Capacity

"Enhance U.S. ability to respond swiftly to biological incidents by modernizing and expanding the footprint of domestic health infrastructure and by restoring public trust in health, science, and medicine, in part by countering misinformation and disinformation."

Target 3.1.4. Strengthen Healthcare-Associated Infections (HAI) and Antibiotic Resistant (AR) Pathogens Capacities

"Ensure states, localities, tribes, and territories can implement comprehensive programs to detect, respond to, and prevent the transmission of healthcare-associated infections (HAI) and antibiotic resistant (AR) pathogens." Specifically, DoD is tasked with leading the following action:

1. "Through E.O. 13676 and the National Action Plan for Combating Antibiotic Resistant Bacteria (CARB), 2020-2025, strengthen U.S. federal and SLTT [state, local, tribal, and territorial] capacity to slow the emergence of resistant bacteria, prevent the spread of resistant infections, promote the responsible use of antibiotics, and conduct surveillance of antibiotic resistant pathogens. (Lead: **DoD**, USDA, HHS, **VA [Department of Veterans Affairs]**; Support: CARB Task Force agencies as identified in the CARB National Action Plan)."

TABLE A.1
NBS Priorities with Actions Assigned to DoD

NBS Goals	Goals Subtype	DoD Leading	DoD Supporting
Goal 1: Enable Risk Awareness and Detection to Inform Decision-Making Across the Biodefense Enterprise	1.1.1. Detection and Reporting of Biological Threats		X
	1.1.2. Biological Threat Sequencing and Analytical Data Sharing		
	1.1.3. Data Integration for Early Warning		X
	1.1.4. Biological Threat Assessment and Characterization Capabilities		X
	1.2. Additional Actions		X
Goal 2: Ensure Biodefense Enterprise Capabilities to Prevent Bioincidents	2.1.2. Establish and Maintain Sustainable Global Financing for Health Security and Pandemic Preparedness		
2.1.1. Strengthen Country Capacities	2.2.1. Promote Safe and Secure Biological Laboratories and Practices		X
	2.2.2. Strengthen Responsible Conduct for Biological Research		X
	2.2.3. Accelerate biosafety and biosecurity innovation		X
	2.2.4. Deter Biological Weapons	X	
	2.2.5. Reduce Zoonotic Pathogen Spillover		

Table A.1—Continued

NBS Goals	Goals Subtype	DoD Leading	DoD Supporting
Goal 3: Ensure Biodefense Enterprise Preparedness to Reduce the Impacts of Bioincidents	3.1.1. Invest in Domestic Public Health Capacities		
	3.1.2. Strengthen Capacities to Combat Emerging and Zoonotic Disease		
	3.1.3. Promote Evidence-Based Health Communication to the Public		
	3.1.4. Strengthen Healthcare-Associated Infections (HAI) and Antibiotic Resistant (AR) Pathogens Capacities	X	
	3.2.1. Pathogen Agnostic Tests		
	3.2.2. Pathogen Specific Tests		
	3.2.3. Rapid, Low Cost, Point-of-Need Tests		X
	3.3.1. PPE Capacity		X
	3.3.2. PPE Innovation		X
	3.4.1. Vaccine Design, Testing, and Authorization		
	3.4.2. Vaccine Production		
	3.4.3. Vaccine Distribution		
	3.4.4. Vaccine Administration and Allocation		
	3.5.1. Therapeutic Development and Manufacturing		X
	3.5.2. Antiviral Development and Manufacturing		

Table A.1—Continued

NBS Goals	Goals Subtype	DoD Leading	DoD Supporting
	3.5.3. Controlling Counterproductive Responses to Infection		X
	3.6. Additional Actions		X
Goal 4: Rapidly Respond to Limit the Impacts of Bioincidents	4.1.1. Effective Response to Mitigate Biological Incidents		X
	4.1.2. Limit Environmental Impacts of Biological Incidents		
	4.1.3. Coordinate Real-Time Research for Response		
	4.1.4. Innovative Clinical-Trial Infrastructure		
Goal 5: Facilitate Recovery to Restore the Community, the Economy, and the Environment after a Bioincident	5.1.1. Recovery Planning and Implementation		

SOURCE: Features information from White House, *National Biodefense Strategy and Implementation Plan for Countering Biological Threats, Enhancing Pandemic Preparedness, and Achieving Global Health Security*, pp. i–xx.
NOTE: Shaded cells = not applicable.

Abbreviations

BW	biological weapons
BWC	Biological and Toxins Weapons Convention
CARB	National Action Plan for Combating Antibiotic Resistant Bacteria
CDC	Centers for Disease Control and Prevention
COVID-19	coronavirus disease 2019
CW	chemical weapons
CWC	Chemical Weapons Convention
DHS	U.S. Department of Homeland Security
DoD	U.S. Department of Defense
DoS	U.S. Department of State
DPRK	Democratic People's Republic of Korea
FBI	Federal Bureau of Investigation
HHS	U.S. Department of Health and Human Services
IC	U.S. Intelligence Community
JCS	U.S. Joint Chiefs of Staff
NBS	National Biodefense Strategy and Implementation Plan
ODNI	U.S. Office of the Director of National Intelligence
OPCW	Organization for the Prohibition of Chemical Weapons
PRC	People's Republic of China
UN	United Nations
UNGA	United Nations General Assembly
UNICRI	United Nations Interregional Crime and Justice Research Institute
UNODA	United Nations Office for Disarmament Affairs
UNSGM	United Nations Secretary-General's Mechanism for Investigation of Alleged Use of Chemical and Biological Weapons
USDA	U.S. Department of Agriculture

References

Alhajj, Mandy, Muhammad Zubair, and Aisha Farhana, "Enzyme Linked Immunosorbent Assay," *StatPearls [Internet]*, April 23, 2023.

Arms Control Association, "Timeline of Syrian Chemical Weapons Activity, 2012–2022," webpage, May 2021. As of June 26, 2023:
https://www.armscontrol.org/factsheets/
Timeline-of-Syrian-Chemical-Weapons-Activity

The Australia Group, "List of Human and Animal Pathogens and Toxins for Export Control," webpage, November 30, 2022. As of July 3, 2023:
https://www.dfat.gov.au/publications/minisite/theaustraliagroupnet/site/en/
human_animal_pathogens.html

Becker-Jakob, Una, "Countering the Use of Chemical Weapons in Syria: Options for Supporting International Norms and Institutions," Stockholm International Peace Research Institute, *EU Non-Proliferation and Disarmament Papers*, No. 63, June 2019.

CDC, HHS, and USDA—*See* Centers for Disease Control and Prevention, U.S. Department of Human and Health Services, and U.S. Department of Agriculture.

Centers for Disease Control and Prevention, U.S. Department of Human and Health Services, and U.S. Department of Agriculture, "Federal Select Agent Program," webpage, August 30, 2022. As of July 3, 2023:
https://www.selectagents.gov/

Chevrier, Marie Isabelle, "Compliance Mechanisms and Their Implementation: The Contrast Between the Biological and Chemical Weapons Conventions," *Nonproliferation Review*, Vol. 27, Nos. 4–6, November 17, 2021.

Clark, William R., "Bioterrorism Beginnings: The Rajneesh Cult, Oregon, 1985," *Oxford University Press's Academic Insights for the Thinking World*, blog, October 5, 2009.

Convention on the Prohibition of the Development, Production and Stockpiling of Bacteriological (Biological) and Toxin Weapons and on Their Destruction (BWC), disarmament treaty, entered into force as of March 26, 1975.

Convention on the Prohibition of the Development, Production, Stockpiling and Use of Chemical Weapons and on their Destruction (CWC), treaty, entered into force as of April 29, 1997.

de Bretton-Gordon, Hamish, "Biosecurity in the Wake of COVID-19: The Urgent Action Needed," *Combating Terrorism Center Sentinel*, Vol. 13, No. 11, November 20, 2020.

Dembek, Zygmunt F., Julie A. Pavlin, Martina Siwek, and Mark G. Kortepeter, "Epidemiology of Biowarfare and Bioterrorism," in Joel Bozue, Christopher K. Cote, and Pamela J. Glass, eds., *Textbooks of Military Medicine: Medical Aspects of Biological Warfare*, Office of the Surgeon General Borden Institute U.S. Army Medical Department Center and School Health Readiness Center of Excellence, 2018.

DoS—*See* U.S. Department of State.

European Centre for Disease Prevention and Control, *Digital Technologies for the Surveillance, Prevention and Control of Infectious Diseases: A Scoping Review of the Research Literature: 2015–2019*, November 16, 2021.

Ghannam, Ryan B., and Stephen M. Techtmann, "Machine Learning Applications in Microbial Ecology, Human Microbiome Studies, and Environmental Monitoring," *Computational and Structural Biotechnology Journal*, Vol. 19, January 27, 2021.

Ghoorchian, Arash, Mahdie Kamalabadi, Zahra Amouzegar, Nahid Rezvani Jalal, Hazem M. Abu Shawish, Salman M. Saadeh, Abbas Afkhami, Tayyebeh Madrakian, Sabu Thomas, Tuan Anh Nguyen, Mazaher Ahmadi, "Chapter 11: Lab-on-a-Chip Miniaturized Analytical Devices," in Sabu Thomas, Mazaher Ahmadi, Tuan Anh Nguyen, Abbas Afkhami, Tayyebeh Madrakian, eds., *Micro- and Nanotechnology Enabled Applications for Portable Miniaturized Analytical Systems*, Elsevier, 2022.

Green, Tyler, "The Mechanisms Behind the United Nations Secretary-General's Mechanism: An Examination of the History and Application of the Fact-Finding Mechanism to the Alleged Chemical Attacks in Syria," *Journal of Biosecurity, Biosafety, and Biodefense Law*, Vol. 10, No. 1, 2019.

Gwinn, Marta, Duncan MacCannell, and Gregory L. Armstrong, "Next-Generation Sequencing of Infectious Pathogens," *JAMA*, Vol. 321, No. 9, March 5, 2019.

JCS—*See* U.S. Joint Chiefs of Staff.

Johansson, Anna-Lena, "Towards a UNSGM Biological Analysis Network: Workshop Report," briefing slides, Swedish Defence Research Agency, June 16–17, 2021.

Jovic, Dragomirka, Xue Liang, Hua Zeng, Lin Lin, Fengping Xu, and Yonglun Luo, "Single-Cell RNA Sequencing Technologies and Applications: A Brief Overview," *Clinical and Translational Medicine*, Vol. 12, No. 3, March 29, 2022.

Katz, Rebecca, Ellie Graeden, Keishi Abe, Aurelia Attal-Juncqua, Matthew R. Boyce, and Stephanie Eaneff, "Mapping Stakeholders and Policies in Response to Deliberate Biological Events," *Heliyon*, Vol. 4, No. 12, December 27, 2018.

Khan, Ali S., Philip S. Amara, and Stephen A. Morse, "Forensic Public Health: Epidemiological and Microbiological Investigations for Biosecurity," in Bruce Budowle, Steven Schutzer, and Stephen Morse, eds., *Microbial Forensics*, Academic Press, 2020.

Knobler, Stacey L., Adel A. F. Mahmoud, and Leslie A. Pray, eds., *Biological Threats and Terrorism: Assessing the Science and Response Capabilities: Workshop Summary*, National Academies Press, 2002.

Koblentz, Gregory D., "Chemical-Weapon Use in Syria Atrocities, Attribution, and Accountability," *Nonproliferation Review*, Vol. 26, Nos. 5–6, February 17, 2020.

Leitenberg, Milton, "False Allegations of Biological-Weapons Use from Putin's Russia," *Nonproliferation Review*, Vol. 27, Nos. 4–6, October 12, 2021.

Lewis, Gregory, Jacob L. Jordan, David A. Relman, Gregory D. Koblentz, Jade Leung, Allan Dafoe, Cassidy Nelson, Gerald L. Epstein, Rebecca Katz, Michael Montague, et al., "The Biosecurity Benefits of Genetic Engineering Attribution," *Nature Communications*, Vol. 11, December 9, 2020.

McDade, Joseph, and David Franz, "Bioterrorism as a Public Health Threat," *Emerging Infectious Diseases*, Vol. 4, No. 3, July–September 1998.

McLeish, Caitríona, and Joshua R. Moon, "Sitting on the Boundary: The Role of Reports in Investigations into Alleged Biological-Weapons Use," *Nonproliferation Review*, Vol. 27, Nos. 4-6, March 12, 2021.

Military Health System and Defense Health Agency, "Electronic Surveillance System for the Early Notification of Community-Based Epidemics," webpage, undated. As of June 28, 2023:
https://www.health.mil/Military-Health-Topics/Health-Readiness/AFHSD/Integrated-Biosurveillance/ESSENCE

Moore, Melinda, Gail Fisher, and Clare Stevens, *Toward Integrated DoD Biosurveillance: Assessment and Opportunities*, RAND Corporation, RR-399-A, 2013. As of June 21, 2023:
https://www.rand.org/pubs/research_reports/RR399.html

Naval Postgraduate School Center for Homeland Defense and Security, "Timeline–Rajneeshee Bioterror Attack," webpage, Homeland Security Digital Library, undated. As of June 28, 2023:
https://www.hsdl.org/c/tl/rajneeshee-bioterror-attack/

ODNI—*See* U.S. Office of the Director of National Intelligence.

OPCW—*See* Organization for the Prohibition of Chemical Weapons.

Organization for the Prohibition of Chemical Weapons, "Incident in Salisbury," webpage, undated. As of June 27, 2023:
https://www.opcw.org/media-centre/featured-topics/incident-salisbury

Organization for the Prohibition of Chemical Weapons, "Responding to the Use of Chemical Weapons," webpage, undated. As of June 27, 2023: https://www.opcw.org/our-work/responding-use-chemical-weapons

Organization for the Prohibition of Chemical Weapons, *Note by the Technical Secretariat: The OPCW in 2025: Ensuring a World Free of Chemical Weapons*, S/1252/2015, March 6, 2015.

Organization for the Prohibition of Chemical Weapons, *Note by the Technical Secretariat: First Report by the OPCW Investigation and Identification Team Pursuant to Paragraph 10 of Decision C-SS-4/Dec.3 'Addressing the Threat From Chemical Weapons Use' Ltamenah (Syrian Arab Republic) 24, 25, and 30 March 2017*, S/1867/2020, April 8, 2020.

Organization for the Prohibition of Chemical Weapons, "OPCW Provides Technical Assistance to Germany Regarding Allegations of Chemical Weapons Use Against Alexei Navalny," press release, September 17, 2020.

Organization for the Prohibition of Chemical Weapons, *Note by the Technical Secretariat: Second Report by the OPCW Investigation and Identification Team Pursuant to Paragraph 10 of Decision C-SS-4/Dec.3 'Addressing the Threat From Chemical Weapons Use' Saraqib (Syrian Arab Republic)–4 February 2018*, S/1943/2021, April 12, 2021.

Organization for the Prohibition of Chemical Weapons, *Analysis of Biotoxins: Report of the Scientific Advisory Board's Temporary Working Group*, Scientific Advisory Board Report SAB/REP/1/23, April 2023.

Organization for the Prohibition of Chemical Weapons, *Note by the Technical Secretariat, Third Report by the OPCW Investigation and Identification Team Pursuant to Paragraph 10 of Decision C-SS-4/Dec.3 'Addressing the Threat From Chemical Weapons Use' Douma (Syrian Arab Republic)–7 April 2018*, S/2125/2023, January 27, 2023.

Organization for the Prohibition of Chemical Weapons Executive Council Document EC-96/NAT.24, "United States of America: Statement by H.E. Ambassador Joseph Manso Permanent Representative of the United States of America to the OPCW at the Ninety-Sixth Session of the Executive Council," March 9, 2021.

Organization for the Prohibition of Chemical Weapons Executive Council Document EC-102/NAT.9, "United States of America: Statement by H.E. Ambassador Joseph Manso Permanent Representative of the United States of America at the OPCW at the 102nd Session of the Executive Council," March 14, 2023.

Perkins, Dana, "International Mechanisms for the Investigation of Alleged Use of Biological Weapons—A Primer," *Army Chemical Review: The Professional Bulletin of the Chemical Corps*, Winter 2018.

Persons, Timothy M., *Science and Tech Spotlight: Genomic Sequencing of Infectious Pathogens*, U.S. Government Accountability Office, GAO-21-426SP, March 30, 2021.

Puig-Serra, Pilar, Maria Cruz Casado-Rosas, Marta Martinez-Lage, Beatriz Olalla-Sastre, Alejandro Alonso-Yanez, Raul Torres-Ruiz, and Sandra Rodriguez-Perales, "CRISPR Approaches for the Diagnosis of Human Diseases," *International Journal of Molecular Sciences*, Vol. 23 No. 3, February 3, 2022.

Quinn, Leanne, "Russia Calls Meeting of Biological Weapons Convention," *Arms Control Today*, Vol. 52, No. 7, September 2022.

Roumpeka, Despoina D., John R. Walllace, Frank Escalettes, Ian Fotheringham, Mick Watson, "A Review of Bioinformatics Tools for Bio-Prospecting from Metagenomic Sequence Data," *Frontiers in Genetics*, Vol. 8, March 6, 2017.

Switzerland Federal Department of Defense Spiez Laboratory, *UNSGM Designated Laboratories Workshop Report*, November 2022.

UN—*See* United Nations.

UNGA—*See* United Nations General Assembly.

UNICRI—*See* United Nations Interregional Crime and Justice Research Institute.

United Nations, "UN Still Sees No Sign of Biological Weapons in Ukraine," October 27, 2022.

United Nations, "UN/Ukraine Biological Weapons," video, November 2, 2022. As of June 26, 2023:
https://www.unmultimedia.org/tv/unifeed/asset/2975/2975545/

United Nations General Assembly Document A/44/561, *Chemical and Bacteriological (Biological) Weapons Report of the Secretary-General*, October 4, 1989.

United Nations General Assembly Document GA/DIS/3666, *Use of Chemical, Biological Weapons Unacceptable in Any Context, Delegates Stress, as First Committee Continues General Debate*, October 7, 2021.

United Nations General Assembly Security Council Document A/67/997-S/2013/553, *Report of the United Nations Mission to Investigate Allegations of the Use of Chemical Weapons in the Syrian Arab Republic on the Alleged Use of Chemical Weapons in the Ghouta Area of Damascus on 21 August 2013*, September 16, 2013.

United Nations General Assembly Security Council Document A/68/663-S/2013/735, *Identical Letters Dated 13 December 2013 from the Secretary-General Addressed to the President of the General Assembly and the President of the Security Council*, December 13, 2013.

United Nations Interregional Crime and Justice Research Institute, *A Prosecutor's Guide to Chemical and Biological Crimes*, May 2022.

United Nations Office for Disarmament Affairs, "Biological Weapons Convention," webpage, undated. As of September 6, 2023: https://disarmament.unoda.org/biological-weapons/

United Nations Office for Disarmament Affairs, "Secretary-General's Mechanism for Investigation of Alleged Use of Chemical and Biological Weapons (UNSGM)," webpage, undated. As of June 26, 2023: https//disarmament.unoda.org/wmd/secretary-general-mechanism

United Nations Office for Disarmament Affairs, "Fact Sheet: The Secretary-General's Mechanism for Investigation of Alleged Use of Chemical and Biological Weapons," fact sheet, January 2023. As of December 6, 2023: https://front.un-arm.org/wp-content/uploads/2023/03/SGM-Fact-Sheet-Jan2023.pdf

UNODA—*See* United Nations Office for Disarmament Affairs.

U.S. Department of State, *Adherence to and Compliance with Arms Control, Nonproliferation, and Disarmament Agreements and Commitments*, April 2023.

U.S. Joint Chiefs of Staff, *Joint Operating Environment (JOE) 2035: The Joint Force in a Contested and Disordered World*, July 14, 2016.

U.S. Joint Chiefs of Staff, "Joint Operating Environment," webpage, undated. As of June 21, 2023: https://www.jcs.mil/Doctrine/Joint-Concepts/JOE/

U.S. Office of the Director of National Intelligence, *Annual Threat Assessment of the U.S. Intelligence Community*, February 2022.

U.S. Office of the Director of National Intelligence, *Annual Threat Assessment of the U.S. Intelligence Community*, February 2023.

U.S. Office of the Director of National Intelligence, *Potential Links Between the Wuhan Institute of Virology and the Origin of the COVID-19 Pandemic*, June 2023.

White House, *National Biodefense Strategy and Implementation Plan for Countering Biological Threats, Enhancing Pandemic Preparedness, and Achieving Global Health Security*, October 2022.

World Organization for Animal Health, *Guidelines for Investigation of Suspicious Biological Events (Guidelines for National Veterinary Services)*, March 2018.